TILT

BY THE SAME AUTHOR

Tattoos for Mother's Day
Hard Water

TILT

Jean Sprackland

CAPE POETRY

Published by Jonathan Cape 2007

4 6 8 10 9 7 5 3

Copyright © Jean Sprackland 2007

Jean Sprackland has asserted her right under the Copyright, Designs
and Patents Act 1988 to be identified as the author of this work

First published in Great Britain in 2007 by
Jonathan Cape
Random House, 20 Vauxhall Bridge Road,
London SW1V 2SA

www.randomhouse.co.uk

Addresses for companies within The Random House Group Limited can be found
at: www.randomhouse.co.uk/offices.htm

The Random House Group Limited Reg. No. 954009

A CIP catalogue record for this book is available from the British Library

ISBN 0224080866

The Random House Group Limited makes every effort to ensure that the
papers used in its books are made from trees that have been legally sourced from
well-managed and credibly certified forests. Our paper procurement policy can
be found at: www.randomhouse.co.uk/paper.htm

Typeset by Palimpsest Book Production Limited, Grangemouth, Stirlingshire
Printed and bound in Great Britain by
William Clowes Ltd, Beccles, Suffolk

for John

Now, on the road to freedom, I was pausing for a moment near Temuco and could hear the voice of the water that had taught me to sing.

Pablo Neruda

CONTENTS

ACKNOWLEDGEMENTS

Acknowledgements are due to the following publications: *Answering Back* (Picador), *Limelight, London Review of Books, New Writing 15* (Granta), *New Yorker, Poetry London, Poetry Review, The Times Literary Supplement.*

The writing of this book has been greatly assisted by an award from Arts Council England, and by time spent at the Tyrone Guthrie Centre at Annaghmakerrig.

I am especially grateful to Robin Robertson for his advice and support.

THE FENCED WOOD

A finger of sunlight points the way
over the floor of dead leaves.
I unlatch the gate and walk in.

I follow the signs:
an acorn
a notched twig
a word written in lichen.

At the centre
a flat stone for a bed.
I lie down to wait.
The cold receives me.
The net of light trembles overhead.

One branch touches the wrist of another.
The breeze catches its breath.

BREAKING THE FALL

Imagine being that fluke of rock
that juts out from the face of the hill,

the rock that breaks the stream's fall,
day and night, for millennia.

The stream runs over, sleek as mercury,
has no choice but to strike you –

shatters into beads that fire away
at more or less predictable angles.

All that varies is the weight of water,
in drought, or after heavy rain;

the pace of the flow; the pitch
and volume of the shattering.

Imagine the deadlock,
the passion. Imagine the stars.

ICE ON THE BEACH

One single sheet of sprung light.
Touched here with the toe of your boot
it hurts in a distant part.

Dream stuff, with its own internal acoustic.
Striking it with a stick raises
a shocked note, a white bruise under the skin –

the physiology of ice on sand
is strange, we have not mapped it.
The sea can only scorch the edge.

This whole bay is locked
under a lid of referred pain.
At one end, a tanker

nudges out of the rivermouth.
In its wash, the ice shelf
barely shivers.

But thirty miles south,
in another town, it creaks
under the pier, where someone kneels,

staring down like a god
through a damaged sky, onto a wilderness
of ridges and blue shadows.

BIRTHDAY POEM

A roll of blue silk
left on the edge of the counter.

Silk. Edge. Under the fluorescent light
that frail equation shimmered. Then

the silk shifted, or the spool relinquished it –

unsleeving
slowly at first, then
gathering confidence
spending itself faster
and faster, a torrent
flashing over and pooling beneath –

and dragged the spool thumping to the floor.
The assistant turned, too late.

Halfway through my life I think of it.
That roll of shining stuff.
Its choice to spill.
Acceleration. Rapture.

SPILT

You took handfuls of sea
to fill the moat of your brother's castle.
First you ran, then went low and steady,
but still it spilt. And you
didn't see this as the fault of the water,
its special talent for escape. To you
this was one more failure
to be shaken off with the weight of childhood.
You shaped the bowl of your hands,
pressed your fingers together,
held it against the sun to check the seal,
crouched in the shallows,
scooped again, again.

And here you are, going low and steady
between your two lives, walking
the impossible street that connects them.
It's dusk. A neighbour
setting bottles on her doorstep
throws you a foreign glance.
And still you arrive
with nothing to offer the people you love
but damp fingers, the evidence.

THE SOURCE

Want to learn the source,
the cool under the surface fire?
Watch the heron:

he snatches the silver voice
from the throat of the river
and swallows it live.

How quick the water heals
and speaks again, how many
darting notes among the reeds.

Follow with your rod and line,
tear a wound
and drag out an echo.

Take home your hoard of silver.
Run a blade along
the seam of the belly,

spill the redblack treasure,
scrape off the mirrorwork.
There. Look. What have you learnt?

The dead reek on the slab.
A small heap of tricks.

TILT

When the wind collapses at last
the sand glitters with oil
like the fine mist of blood
a dying man would breathe
onto his friend's face and shirt.

It's this freak weather.
For five days and five nights the storm
hacked the steel legs, mauled the derricks.
The pipes flailed and shuddered.
Nothing the men could do
but play blackjack and drink the rig dry.

He has his friend by the sleeves
but he's losing his grip.

The word was not spill, but *incident*.

II

The birds calibrate, re-calibrate
the grains of magnetite in their heads
against their star-maps,
their clock of polarised sunlight –
but it's no good, south is cancelled.

Infrasound, dead-reckoning
are not enough. They fall like hail
on the Atlantic, the Sahara,
the High Tatras, the shocked
roof gardens of Manhattan.

III

What we're seeing is something immense
but distant, a galactic event,
a cosmic wobble, a glitch
on the Milankovitch Cycle.
The earth nudged off its axis
like a wheel skewed on its axle. See,

our planet is bored and oblique. It sits
on the lip of the dark. Then flick!
Like a needle skipping the groove.
Oh dear, I'm showing my age.
Let me put it another way:

the maths was slightly out.
We'd been working on old assumptions
and flawed equations. Twenty-one point five
to twenty-four point five degrees. Poor old earth,

didn't give it much latitude.
Same weary ellipse. Same old axial tilt.
Now it's free to discover its own inclination –

Pardon? Good question.
Straight answer: we don't know.
But theoretically,
everything.

IV

When you slide along my already
slick and unreliable surfaces,

you remind me I am liquid,
you make me care about nothing except
falling, spilling, flooding.

All ice wants to be water.

Listen –

that sound at the edge of the dark
is the world's ice ticking.

V

The city wakes to a tearing sound:
the ocean gathering itself,

mustering its goods: fish, whales,
luminous monsters with no names,

cruiseships, crashed aeroplanes, corpses
weighed down with stones,

drowned forests and volcanoes,
fibre optics, crude oil, spent reactors, each thing

sucked from its hiding place, and the sea
scouring its own floor, even the rifts and fissures,

dragging out the last flakes of life
and then fistfuls of utter dark,

all jacked high on the storm,
kicked over the city, right over the watching streets –

a mixed catch, writhing
in a green net of water.

VI

A partly dismantled giraffe.
A row of rat enclosures.
A zebra which can only sweat
and stare at its own hooves.

The zookeeper's shovel
rusting against a wall.
His special coat all spidery
on its hook in the feed store.

The thrum of an electric fence.
The air like glue.

Enter a stray cat
with a baby monkey in its jaws.

COWS

Over the shrug of the motorway bridge
they go, their vintage design
stirring vague pangs of grief
in salesmen and long-distance lorry drivers.

As a child I would scramble under the hedge
to consult with cows. I found them enigmatic
with their slow conversation, lathery breath,
eyes like planets. It seemed they had few plans,
gave scant thought to the question of destiny.
But sometimes there might be a calf,
with soft hooves and a stunned expression –
a dumb prophet, visited by this future:

no dry-straw jostle of the cowshed,
no shuck-and-thud of the milking machine,
just the keening road, and the ghost cattle
crossing from nowhere to nowhere.

FEELINGS

He adjusted the chain on my bike, so I let him
leave a few oily marks on my blouse. After that

he'd always be coming round when my parents were out,
asking how did I feel. Had my feelings
grown, altered or faded. Were they dying.

I thought of a tortoise asleep in a box of straw.
In spring you had to reach in and feel for warmth,
carry it onto the grass and try it with dandelions.

It was weeks before I knew that all I wanted
was to be driven at night up to the gravel pit
wearing only his proper coat, then to throw it off
and run into the water feeling nothing at all.

HANDS

She peels cod fillets off the slab,
dips them in batter, drops them
one by one into the storm of hot fat.
I watch her scrubbed hands,
elegant at the work

and think of the hands of the midwife
stroking wet hair from my face as I sobbed and cursed,
calling me Sweetheart and wheeling in more gas,
hauling out at last my slippery fish of a son.
He was all silence and milky blue. She took him away
and brought him back breathing,
wrapped in a white sheet. By then
I loved her like my own mother.

I stand here speechless in the steam and banter,
as she makes hospital corners of my hot paper parcel.

ESCAPE

From your room on the top floor
of the cheap hotel, it's a crazy sight:
a clutter of rusty ladders and rails,
bolted together, dithering in the wind.

Escher-style it zig-zags down
approximate to the rickety brickwork,
rooted (you assume) in the hinterland
of wheely-bins and old fridges.

When you look again
it's Meccano: no more reliable
than the boats and cranes
and time-machines you built as a child.

The only one who risks it is the engineer
on the annual check (you hope), testing
for metal fatigue and loose nuts.
Don't pause to imagine these

when the flames come rocketing up the stairwell
and kick the door off its hinges,
hyperactive on foam furniture.
Wrestle the jammed sash and step out

game and naked over the two-foot gap.
This is no time to wonder, as it creaks
and slews, shouldn't there be
a fire escape escape?

THIRD DAY OF THE HONEYMOON

She gets up before he wakes,
finds her dress inside-out on the floor,
puts on plastic shoes and goes down to the sea.

Sex has emptied her, she's forgetting to eat.
Salt cold rinses her sleek and girlish again,
raises bumps on her hairtrigger skin.
She jumps the waves, pulling faces
because no one's watching her.

The water licks and smacks, and it happens
quick as the word yes: the wedding band's tugged
over the knuckle and off.
She pulls up a few bunches of water, but really
she knows it's gone, glinting like a trick
somewhere down there in the shift
and tangle of deep life.

Later he'll kiss the thin white place, say
Never mind, I'll buy you another.
For now, she's properly naked at last.

CATCH ME

Hold a warm condom to the light
to see the fund of life inside.

Not so long ago
the only place to hold this was the body,
its channels and propagation chambers,
and pleasure was taken ripe with consequence.

And once there were no vessels
and no containment.
No fashioning of wood or stone
into a jug to carry water –
water had to be visited, drunk where it lived,
paths marked to those holy places.
No rooms to fill with music,
no music to carry longing or grief
but wind, thunder, animal cries.

Then came the mud house,
the leaky bowl of leaves.
We learned like children to keep and store,
to build edges and own space.
And later one of us said to the other
I'm everywhere, I'm lost, catch me,
make your arms into walls and hold me.

A PHONE OFF THE HOOK

Left for five minutes
it starts up a wail, a siren,
its own private emergency.

It's the agony
of being left like this, open
but with the connection broken.

It would rather have whatever
you might spit or whisper into it
than this. The receiver put down wrong,

balanced at a bad angle
like a broken bone,
and no one coming to mend it.

THE MAP IS NOT THE TERRITORY

(Alfred Korzybski)

The pirates would swarm aboard
slashing throats and seizing the maps.
Without maps, all the black pepper, all the slaves
might as well be thrown into the sea.

But maps could lie. Under the spitting lantern
the mapmaker practised a dark art,
drawing up insurance against loss.
Invented a safe route onto lethal rocks.
Marked a green island where there was nothing
but empty blue road under a ratcheting sun.

Unthinkable now, we are so correct
with our clean atlas of distant starfields

and even the body mapped –
its fabric unpicked, its algorithms read,
every nub and rubric imaged and modelled,
down to the last glisten of stuff.

Each of our diagrams is as true
as we know how to make it.
No trap street, no bit of bad code.

So how will we hold something back
when they board us and raid us?

FOGBOUND

It leaks in at the window
he always insists on having open.
It drifts and smoulders,

smudges the edges of their
twin breathing, seeps through their dreams
like milk spreading through water.

The bed, offshore by now, drifting
beyond the range of foghorn and lighthouse,
slides into blind navigation.

Such casual dead-reckoning
as sleep allows
gives false bearings, and by now

it's white-out.
The dressing-table mirror
sweats, reflecting nothing.

With daylight
they dock at last in clear air.
She rolls to find him

but it's too late.
No salvage but silence.
The sheets like ice.

MIRACLES

The sea was bucking and snapping
but his feet made a road across it.

I came straight here when I heard. By then
the waves themselves were talking.
They said they were changed forever. They said

he could have bulldozed it with some heavy ship,
broken it in a motorboat, revved up the engine
and strimmed it flat,

but he steadied the boat and stepped out.
The sole of his foot was like a cool hand
on a burning forehead.

I was ready to throw myself in, I'd have drowned
just to kiss those feet. But I was too late.

No one there but a surfer
walking the high sandbank
a hundred yards out from shore.

II HEALED

I was a locked garden till he came along,
a fountain sealed, etc.

So he tells me. But it wasn't my idea.
The crowd pushed me forward
and he touched my ears, my lips.
There was grit in the clay.
I don't need your thanks, he says,
but at least stop scrabbling in the dirt,
it's not reversible.

They say I was a strange child:
stood at the same window all day,
reading jet-trail diagrams, counting
clockwork flies winding down on the sill.

Now I'm like a newborn baby
screaming for the womb. Or a fish
thrashing on the deck,
begging so hard for the water
you kick it back in.

Anyhow, he says, *that's my show.*
My spit, my fingers, me.
I'm blinded by voices. My tongue tastes of him.

I was awkward in my white silk.
His aunts talked too fast,
no one knew my language.

I wish I could say I saw it change as he poured.
All I know is we drank from the same glass
and I forgot to be shy.

Easy for you to say *trick*.
I led him upstairs and he tore off my dress.
We lay down together and spoke in tongues.

I learnt his demotic: *Now*.
The glass drained and slammed on the bar.

And I taught him my own:
Slow down. Gentle. Wait.
The wine held and warmed in the mouth.

IV A DRAUGHT OF SONGBIRDS

When he came to the square to address the crowd
the mood was desperate.
There had been a helicopter drop
but it was only blankets and polythene.

He watched as the mob threw bottles, then petrol bombs.
A looter was dragged from a house and lynched.
We raised our Kalashnikovs
but he said *Wait* –

and a shoal of birds swam overhead
and we sprayed it with holes.
We reaped the sky, and the hungry people
gathered the shattered birds in their coats.

At market, in better days,
five of these would sell for a few pence.
Yet he stood in the bloodstained square and wept
where feathers fell around him like snow.

V SIGHTING

I'm killing time at the services.
He's cross-legged on the bridge,
the M6 shuddering beneath him.

I wish I was in the shop, picking out
a road atlas of the British Isles,
an inflatable pillow, a keyring. I try to walk by

but he lifts his T-shirt and shows me
the blue of spoilt meat, the gleam of bone.
I'd throw him some coins but I know
that's not it. He wants me to touch.

I'll say it. Whatever it takes.
It's all right, I believe you. I know who you are.

Then quickly over to the slot machines
and the bad coffee. Try out the massage chair.
Print business cards for a business I haven't got.

VI EXORCISED

There's a demon that makes you nothing but cunt.
Your baby howls for milk behind a closed door
while you do this thing, do it, do it,

you're helpless, staked to this man.
But then he takes another, and you must
set fire to her house, pull off her head

or stave in her eyes with your fingers.
Next comes the terror of knowing for sure
that the axis is skewed,

the planets are making random orbits.
You breathe all wrong, the floor tilts and slithers,
your lungs burst with someone else's filthy words,

and the women catch you in their strong arms,
though you bite and curse them. They take you
to the priest, who starts a spell,

and raises his hand, a cross, a charm,
which before your eyes grows a mouth
with intent little teeth. It darts

with savage delicacy into your mouth,
tugs a rope of scalding rags,
drags gagging out of your throat into the open

a winged creature, charring the air.
It spits and flashes, shakes itself free
of the prayerwords, then flies.

You lie at the feet of your priest,
in a pool of his light, which is all gentleness now.
He reaches down a cool hand.

And pushing aside the women who held you –
those women who stroked you
and sang to you – pushing them aside, you seize it.

MATTRESSES

Tipped down the embankment, they
sprawl like sloshed suburban wives,

buckled and split, slashed by rain,
moulded by bodies dead or disappeared
and reeking with secrets.

A lineside museum of sleep and sex,
an archive of thrills and emissions,
the histories of half-lives
spent hiding in the dark.

Arthritic iron frames might still be worth a bit,
but never that pink quilted headboard,
naked among thistles, relic
of some reckless beginning, testament

to the usual miracle: the need to be close,
whatever the stains or the bruises.

BARN OWL

We lay in a hurricane
under the roof of its wings

trapped inside the engine-house
of their beating

We were naked in the heat
Its claws could have torn us apart

It was an annunciation
that smelt of stars and dead mice

I had been dreaming of clocks
and a muddle of keys that should wind them

A scuffle, you calling Who's that?
and the storm broke over us

PHYSICS

By every rule in the book
I should be dead. Instead
I'm frozen in this hall of blue light,
wavy lines, blunt silence.
My arms are bleached bones
stuck in a kung-fu pose.
I watch my fingernails, but they don't grow.

Somewhere inside me,
a baffled clock ticks on. Where's the boy
who played *sleeping with the fishes*?
He shinned down the swimming-pool wall, blowing
slow bubbles, lay on the bottom
counting eight nine ten . . . he loved
to be bearing the weight of all that water.
Say I'd once had a wife, would she still think of me?
What news of the child we might have expected?

I heard that before the Big Bang
there was no such thing as time.
I didn't believe it then.
I'm unfastened in the amnesiac cold
and the one clear thing I know I had and lost
is the flex of the diving-board under my feet,
the lovely air
curving and following through.

ALARM

How many times have I reached
through the soft hatch between worlds
to tap the stop button?

At night the bed grows and sprawls,
I roam its many small addresses,

yet the same digital pulse always brings me back.
I try my clogged voice,
my butterfly fists. Rub grit from my eyes.

The plastic face is a mirror
reflecting my own choices

though it insists on translating them
into square, and flashing,
and twenty-four-hour clock.

It's a throwaway item, the sort
that comes free with so many reams of paper,

yet when I'm travelling so light
I've shucked off everything –
shoes, tickets, baby, even my name –

it hauls me back to where my children live,
older, and fewer, and scarred only

by brambles and vaccination.
They stand around the bed, waiting
for ordinary things like food and money,

demanding to know right now
whether I believe in life after death.

DRIED FISH

The Japanese fishmonger shook his head when I asked for a name, but I took it home anyway and she unwrapped it sighing *This is hard as the sole of a boot* but she put it to soak while I opened wine, sliced fennel, weighed out white beans, and yes I did hear something, tap dripping that's what I thought, then we started in on the wine and I watched her bend to fetch candles from the back of a cupboard, it had been so long, and I told her that joke, you know the one, contortionist, snake-charmer, made it dirtier, funnier, god I was eloquent tonight, and I scrabbled in a drawer for a squashed Marlboro packet, one left so we shared it, the taste of her lipstick made me dizzy, and true at the edge of my eye I thought something twitched, something silver, but now she was opening her dress, and my hands were remembering their way, the table creaking beneath us like a boat, fennel rusting against the knife, white beans scattered like pebbles, I pushed inside her, she made an astonished sound from a previous life, and that's when I saw it, the fish on the draining board, leaping, drowning a second time, leaping, mouthing the same mistake

HIJACKED

When he can bring himself to go back to work
he pays the carpenter to double-bolt the coffins.

He tells no one. Who'd believe him?
The creak of the lid in the back of the hearse,
the sudden whiff of Jeyes Fluid. Then
the cracked ice of that voice. *Take me to the airport.*

MACHINERY

I had forgotten that word –
it leaves a hot taste on the tongue.
These days the old religion is mentioned only
by lunatics and academics.

But a word, like a lost tooth, leaves a gap
that will never close completely.

And there are others:
Girder. Tarmac. *Interface.*

THE STOPPED TRAIN

She stands and knows herself for the first time.
This recognition comes to each of us

sooner or later. When a baby meets a mirror
it enters this same state of rapture.
That's how the train is: stunned
and passionate. She looks, and sees

energy, will, destiny. Sees that she
touches the rails, but is not the rails,
brushes the overhead lines and drinks in power,
is headstrong and pioneering.

Inside, passengers cram the corridors,
sucking ice-cubes, taking turns at the windows.
A woman shouts: Why must you all be so *British*?
The carriage is brash with daylight

like a terrible living-room
filling up with unsaid things:
no one can get a signal here
in this nondescript England of

sly ditches and flat fields, where some
experiment must be taking place and
the only thing moving between the trees is
shadow. This is the Interior,

and if they were to smash the glass with a shoe,
jump down onto the track, set off in a somewhere
    direction,
they would be struck down
like stranded motorists in Death Valley.

The train has forgotten them.
She is accounting for herself:
steel, glass, plastic, nylon,
an audit of chips and circuits.

She stands and ticks,
letting the heat leak and equalise.

BRACKEN

Lives by its own rules, obeys
a single imperative: *Swarm*

Can smell the space a mile away
where trees have been cleared

Claims squatters' rights
from Norway to Tasmania

and has been seen through telescopes
on the surface of Venus

Closes over the heads of children
where they lie waiting to be found

Spins long curled arguments
tentative as fists

that drink in confidence
thicken into dogma

grow brown and esoteric
waiting for the moment

to pounce on the accident
of the discarded match

THE DEAL

He grins and pulls back his sleeve to show
his arm loaded and glinting with cheap watches.

Without a word, he suggests this transaction:
a handful of leaves in exchange for something
he swears on his mother's grave is gold
and comes with a three-year guarantee.
He'll unfasten it from his own arm and strap it,
with its charge of body-warmth, to my wrist.
His fingers are blunt, but he will try to be gentle.

I stand for a long time, looking at all
the trapped faces, the hands moving in synch.
I've never seen such cruelty, such consensus.
I get him to turn and turn his arm. Broken light
shivers over the metal and glass.
I say I would like to touch. He says nothing.

CAPTIONS

We are described
in the language of rain on a train window –
not running down the glass, but lashed across it.

Awkward text, hammered out
against the direction of travel, almost
too jumpy, too broken to read.

Out there is where we meet,
two inarticulate ghosts on the screen of the night.
It's the only way we can look at each other.

The captions punch and stammer over us.
I watch you blink. I watch you watch me blink.

YOU

You who have taken me stumbling and refusing
to the brink, and eased me over;
you who saw the gown pulled off,
the grey face gaping, deadweight limbs
thumping back on the table;
you with your intimate poisons and devices,
watching my progress as I dived down
into the foreign rivers of my own blood;
you vigilant ones, who monitored depth and velocity,
ready if needed to push me further, ready at last
to reach in and pull me out: you are marvellous
who have each time hauled me up,
brought me thrashing to the surface, ravenous
with grief and gratitude.

THE BIRKDALE NIGHTINGALE

(Bufo calamito – the Natterjack toad)

On Spring nights you can hear them
two miles away, calling their mates
to the breeding place, a wet slack in the dunes.
Lovers hiding nearby are surprised
by desperate music. One man searched all night
for a crashed spaceship.

For amphibians, they are terrible swimmers:
where it's tricky to get ashore, they drown.
By day they sleep in crevices under the boardwalk,
run like lizards from cover to cover
without the sense to leap when a gull snaps.
Yes, he can make himself fearsome,
inflating his lungs to double his size.
But cars on the coast road are not deterred.

She will lay a necklace of pearls in the reeds.
Next morning, a dog will run into the water and scatter them.
Or she'll spawn in a footprint filled with salt rain
that will dry to a crust in two days.

Still, when he calls her and climbs her
they are well designed. The nuptial pads on his thighs
velcro him to her back. She steadies beneath him.

The puddle brims with moonlight.
Everything leads to this.

THREE VOICES

I thought they were sand, shifting and sighing.
I thought they were marram-grass
brushing the hand of the night.

Build me a house out of bones, said the first.
I don't care if the wind rattles through it,
if the windows are smashed
and the hallway is littered with needles.

A boat, said another. *Bring me a boat made of hair,*
no matter how leaky, how scuppered.
I must have a boat or I'm nothing.

Then closer, a third: *Lend me your coat of skin.*
It's a shred of a coat, and you only wear it
from habit, or weariness. Lend it to me.

The path was tripwired with bramble,
deadlocked with buckthorn.
I crashed through and ran
for the shivering lights that were home.

THREE LAKES

I

The lake had been drained that night
and filled with sky instead.

We stood on the jetty
as if on a summit, looking down
on a fathomless depth of cloud.

Sky overhead,
sky at our feet

like deep past
and deep future

and we stood halfway between.

It was one ten in the morning.
I can't remember who stood there with me.

II

Its green complacency makes him cruel.
He tramps the shoreline, glaring at reflections,
demanding to see some depth for Christ's sake.

A breeze raises temporary frowns
like a dream creasing a smooth brow.
It's all surface! Doesn't know how to suffer

like a tree split open by lightning,
a field ploughed and left undone in the rain.
Nothing here but elegant dimples and ripples,

a conceited little repertoire
of sucking and slapping sounds.
And whatever he does, he can't seem to wound it –

a rock makes only brief scattering circles;
heave in a shopping trolley, an old fridge,
it heals around, through, over.

But drive into the shallows and open the sump
and the oil spreads and sheens
into sudden rainbows. He sees at once

this is love not hate after all.
Shuddering he strips and parts the lake.
His feet find sharp and slippery mysteries

as he flails from the bank
and makes for open water,
the slick of fridge coolant and dead oil.

III

You jolt awake from the dream of your life,
gasping at the here-and-now.
Stones underfoot then mud then nothing.
You're fastened in a heavy collar of ice.
The water slakes its thirst on your blood-warmth.

That may not be weed brushing your thigh.
Under this green lid, a lost topography
of caves and thickets, tenanted by ancients.
The drowned swimmer the locals speak of,
still clutching his letters of introduction.

Perfect sky: low and smoky with rain.
The lake bruised and choppy, a nervous current.
You shove against it, knowing you're alive,
knowing that someday soon you'll die.
You open the surface a moment, it shuts behind you.

FIREBREAK

You can follow me deep into the forest
but you can't cross this corridor of air.

The flames thrash at nothing,
the cool repels them.

The warp and weft of gnats and light rain.
The blaze of you, so close it hurts.

THE WAY DOWN

Forget the path.
Hack through gorse and blackthorn
and walk into the stream.

The thing about a stream is
it knows where it's going, has a gift
for finding the shortest route.

A path can lose its nerve,
peter out into bog or bracken, divide
inscrutably in two. I've stood at that place

and weighed the choices, weighed
and checked again, while mist crawls
over the mountain like sleep.

When the stream divides
both streamlets are equally sure.
Each plays its own game – the slick of moss,

the sudden race over a sill of rock –
and each, if you let it,
will carry you down.

THAW

From the helicopter he sees at last
anomalies in the pattern of melt.
The snow has turned informer.

It must have seemed the perfect accomplice,
erasing everything, the way a quilt
might be thrown over a wrecked bed.

Earth was another – tons of it,
shovelled by hand and then by machine,
a loan from the building site
where somebody's cousin worked –

and time, of course. The wound
closed, scabbed over. In summer
there was rough grass, yellow flowers,
even butterflies.

Circle again, he says, and hears
his own voice cracking and slipping.
He reads the diagram of broken snow.
He'll need to radio down, get it ground-truthed.
They'll peel back the scab,
expose what everyone knows already:

under the heaviest winter, the stash of warmth.

THE ENGINE

When I walked away after being with him
I turned the world with my feet.

Me and my incalculable strength.
I kicked the city pavement
and set the world spinning.
It was mass, it was cold and inert
and I was the engine.

I knew just how hard to kick,
how fast to turn it. I was all
energy and restraint, drive and precision.

I was loved, and the earth had no claim on me –
it could not keep me or break me,
could not open and swallow me.
I held it with my powerful feet
as an eagle holds a lamb,

but I would never harm it.
I was a force for good.
I moved invisibly through the crowd,

breathing in the spoilt air
and breathing it out clean.